福兰课教授 STEAM 科学教育

第一册

Professor Frank's STEAM Science Education (Volume I)

[美] 福兰课 (Francis Wallace Stonier) 主编

高林莲　黄笑然 译

西南大学出版社
SWUP
国家一级出版社 全国百佳图书出版单位

图书在版编目（CIP）数据

福兰课教授 STEAM 科学教育 . 第一册 / (美) 福兰课 (Francis Wallace Stonier) 主编 ; 高林莲 , 黄笑然译 . 重庆 : 西南大学出版社 , 2024. 12. -- ISBN 978-7-5697-2758-6

Ⅰ . G613.3

中国国家版本馆 CIP 数据核字第 2024LP8374 号

福兰课教授 STEAM 科学教育（第一册）

FULANKE JIAOSHOU STEAM KEXUE JIAOYU (DI-YI CE)

[美] 福兰课 (Francis Wallace Stonier) 主编　高林莲　黄笑然 译

策划编辑	王　宁　陈　郁
责任编辑	陈　郁　文佳馨
责任校对	王　宁
装帧设计	散点设计
插　　画	周骏勇　陈超超
出版发行	西南大学出版社（原西南师范大学出版社）
	地址：重庆市北碚区天生路 2 号
	邮编：400715
印　　刷	重庆升光电力印务有限公司
成品尺寸	215 mm x 270 mm
印　　张	3.5
字　　数	138 千字
版　　次	2024 年 12 月第 1 版
印　　次	2024 年 12 月第 1 次印刷
书　　号	ISBN 978-7-5697-2758-6
定　　价	38.00 元

编委会

作者简介

福兰课（Francis Wallace Stonier），教育专家，美国桥水学院学前教育学、教育心理学双学士，佐治亚州立大学工商管理硕士，西佐治亚州立大学地理信息系统硕士，欧道明大学教育学博士。曾任五年美国小学科学教师，西佐治亚州立大学终身教授，有二十多年的一线教学经验。

目录 CONTENTS

你了解 STEAM 吗?

本书包含了科学(Science),技术(Technology),工程(Engineering),艺术(Art)和数学(Math)多领域学科的相关的内容。STEAM 是一种以孩子容易接受的方式去教授他们科学的方法，旨在打破各个学科之间的界限，将它们整合在一起去更好地解决问题。在学完了这本书后，您应该会注意到，并非所有的跨学科主题活动都会涉及 STEAM 的 5 个方面，这是正常的。您只需要知道，STEAM 的所有方面都可以跟科学这一大主题相结合。书中所包含的 12 项跨学科活动涵盖了自然、光、太空等广泛的科学主题。与之配套的操作手册，可以帮助家长和教育工作者们，以孩子为中心的方式去更好地开展书中的各项活动。所有的活动都需要孩子亲自动手操作，这能让他们体验到很多学习的乐趣。我希望孩子们能在您的带领下，对科学学习和动手实践产生更加浓厚的兴趣！

This book contains introductions on a wide variety of science, technology, engineering, art, and math (STEAM) activities. STEAM is a means of exposing young learners to science concepts in approachable ways. Subjects do not need to be taught in isolation but can be integrated together. You will notice that not all STEAM activities address all 5 aspects of STEAM every time. This is normal, but all elements of STEAM fall under the umbrella of science. The 12 activities in the book cover a wide range of topics including nature, light and space. The instructions provided are aimed at helping parents and educators to conduct these activities in a more child-centered way as these are hands-on activities that should engage children's interest in learning in a fun way. I hope you enjoy sharing this knowledge with the children you work with and it will help foster a love of hands-on learning and a greater interest in science!

01 栖息地：沙漠和苔原

Habitats: Desert and Tundra

你知道吗
Do you know

我们将探索两种截然不同的栖息地——沙漠和北极苔原。

首先，让我们来看看沙漠吧。沙漠遍布全球，有时候会很热，有时候会很冷。热沙漠的特点是地面几乎完全被沙子覆盖，干旱少雨，白天气温极高。

在沙漠中，仙人掌是最常见的植物之一，种类多样，形态各异。此外，沙漠还是兔子、骆驼和老鼠等哺乳动

物的家园。在沙漠中，还可以看到蛇、陆龟和蜥蜴等爬行动物在沙中穿行；而蜘蛛、蝎子和甲虫等动物也在此栖息。沙漠的天空上，还有猫头鹰、鹰和秃鹫等鸟类在翱翔。许多动物选择在夜晚气温较低时出来活动，你还知道哪些动物生活在沙漠中呢？

Today, we're going to explore two very different habitats: the desert and the Arctic tundra. Let's start with the desert!

Frist, let's take a look at the desert. Deserts can be found all over the world. They can be either hot or cold. A hot desert is defined as an area with very little precipitation, where the ground is almost entirely covered by sand. And hot deserts can be extremely hot during the day.

Cacti are among the most common plants in the desert. They come in a wide variety of shapes and sizes!

Mammals such as rabbits, camels, and mice inhabit the desert.

Reptiles like snakes, tortoises, and lizards navigate through the sand.

Insects and arachnids, including spiders, scorpions, and beetles, crawl around.

Birds such as owls, hawks, and vultures soar above the desert.

Many animals become active at night when it's cooler. Can you think of any other animals that live in the desert?

接下来，让我们转向北极苔原。这种被称为北极苔原的栖息地，气候寒冷，冰雪覆盖。苔原之上，树木寥寥无几，主要生长着草、灌木和苔藓等小型植物。

在北极苔原，驯鹿、北极狐和北极熊在广阔的土地上漫步。北极燕鸥和雪鸮等鸟类在这片冰冷的土地上筑巢生息。独角鲸和海豹等生物在周围的海洋中自由游弋。你还知道北极苔原上有哪些生物呢？

Next, let's turn to the Arctic tundra.

These habitats, known as the Arctic tundra, are extremely cold and are characterized by their ice and snow coverage.

The Arctic tundra has very few trees. Only small plants like grass, shrubs, and moss can grow there.

Reindeer, Arctic foxes, and polar bears wander these lands.

Birds like terns, and owls make their homes in these cold territories.

Narwhals, and seals swim in the oceans.

What other creatures live in the Arctic tundra?

动手创作吧
Maker Space

来了解一下热沙漠和北极苔原栖息地中独特的生命吧！

Let's learn about the unique life in hot desert and Arctic tundra habitats!

互动小游戏
Interactive Games

你可以任意说出一种沙漠或者苔原栖息地中的动物或植物，孩子们可以抢答它属于动物还是植物，是生活在热沙漠还是北极苔原栖息地。比如，老师说：“蛇！”孩子们应该回答：“动物！沙漠！”如果想让游戏更好玩，可以分组进行抢答。

You can name any animal or plant from a desert or tundra habitat, and the kids can identify whether it is an animal or a plant, as well as whether it lives in a hot desert or an icy tundra quickly. For example, the teacher says: “ Snakes” ! The kids should answer: “ Animal! Desert!” If you want to make the game more entertaining, play it in groups.

科学小课堂
Science Tips

北极熊在冬天为什么要睡大觉呢？因为冬天的北极很冷，而且黑夜很长，北极熊找食物变得很难。北极熊最爱吃的海豹，会游到别的地方去，北极熊找不到它们了。因为很冷，北极熊需要的能量也多，为了保持体力，北极熊就会选择长时间睡觉，这样它们不需要太多的食物就可以度过寒冷的冬天。

Why do polar bears sleep in winter? Polar bears have a hard time finding food in the Arctic throughout the winter since it is so cold and dark. The seals, the bear's favorite food, will swim somewhere else, and the bears can't find them. Polar bears require a lot of energy due to the extreme cold, so they sleep for long periods of time to maintain their strength. In this way, they may go through the long, hard winter without eating much food.

科学关键词
Science Key Words

栖息地： 生物生存和繁衍的地方称为栖息地。

Habitat: The natural environment which supports the survival and reproduction of the living things.

哺乳动物： 脊椎动物哺乳纲动物的统称。

Mammal: Mammals are vertebrate animals constituting the class Mammalia.

苔原： 极地或高山永久冻土分布区，主要植物有地衣和苔藓等。

Tundra: A large flat area or mountainous area with permanently frozen subsoil that only supports low growing plants such as lichen, moss and so on.

02 指纹艺术

Fingerprint Art

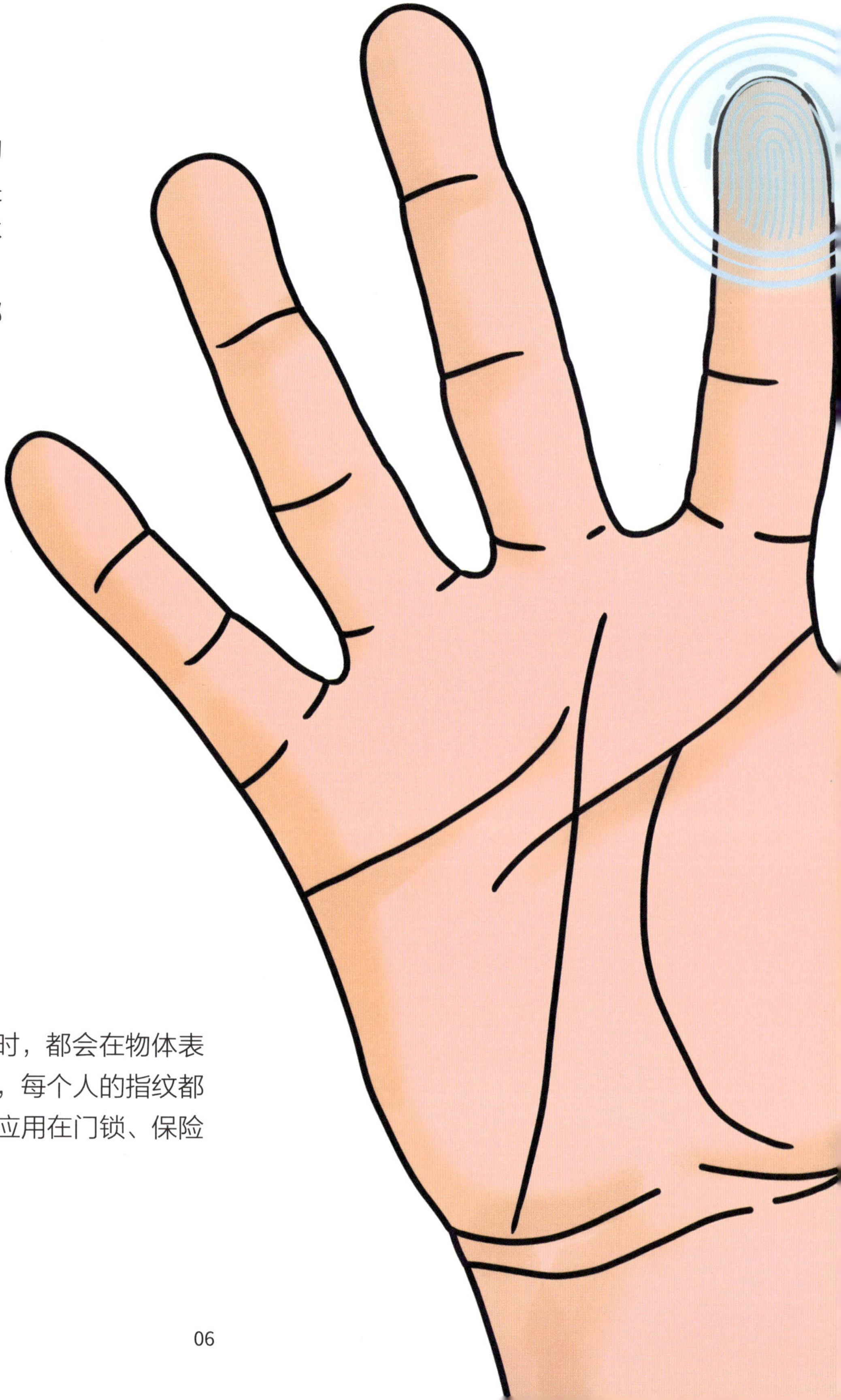

你知道吗 Do you know

观察一下你手指指尖上的纹理，这些独特的图案就是你的指纹。指纹有三种基本形状：箕型、斗型和弓型。你能识别出你的指纹属于哪一种吗？

我们每次用手指触碰物体时，都会在物体表面留下自己的指纹。有趣的是，每个人的指纹都是独一无二的，因此，指纹被应用在门锁、保险箱和手机等的生物识别锁上。

Take a look at the ends of your fingers. Look at the patterns on your fingertips, these are your fingerprints!

Fingerprints come in 3 different main styles: loops, whorls, or arches. Which one do you have?

When we touch things with our fingers, we leave a fingerprint behind.

Did you know that everyone has their own unique or special fingerprint?

Because everyone's fingerprint is their own, we can use fingerprints for locks on doors, safes, and phones! This kind of lock is a biometric lock.

Sometimes police use fingerprints to help find criminals if they left fingerprints at the scene of the crime! This kind of detective work could be called forensics.

In addition to the application in the field of security and law, we can also use fingerprints to create art and enjoy the fun of fingerprints.

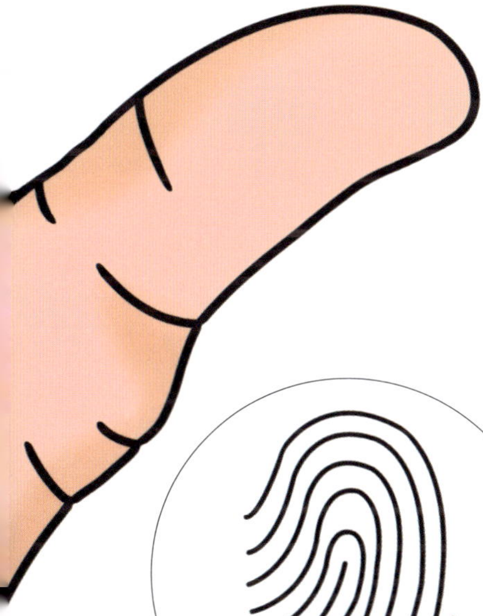

如果犯罪现场留有犯罪者的指纹，警察就可以利用这些指纹找到犯罪者。

除了在安全和法律领域的应用外，我们还可以用指纹来进行艺术创作，享受指纹带来的乐趣。

动手创作吧
Maker Space

今天，就让我们更仔细地观察自己的指纹，并用它们来进行一些艺术创作吧！

Today, let's take a closer look at our fingerprints and then let's create some art with them!

互动小游戏
Interactive Games

伸出你的手指来！其他小朋友可以说出任意一只手的一根手指的名称，听到指令后，你快速伸出对应的手指。例如，指令：左手食指！则快速伸出左手的食指。

Stretch your fingers! Other kids can call out the name of one finger on either hand, and when you hear the command, quickly extend the corresponding finger. For example, when they call out "left index finger", you should swiftly stretch out the index finger of your left hand.

科学小课堂
Science Tips

指纹是每个人特有的标志，就像地球上没有两片完全相同的雪花一样。科学家发现，世界上出现两个一模一样的指纹的概率是150 亿分之一，也就是说，几乎不可能存在一模一样的指纹！这些独一无二的图案在我们还在妈妈肚子里时就形成了，一生都不会改变。即使手指受伤，指纹还是会按照原来的模式长回来。因为这个原因，指纹也叫做“人体身份证”，是我们每个人最特别的密码。

Similar to how no two snowflakes are alike on Earth, every person's fingerprints are unique. Scientists discovered that the possibility of two identical fingerprints in the world is one in 15 billion, making it nearly impossible for an identical one to exist! These distinct fingerprints appear while we are still in our mothers' wombs and remain constant throughout our lives. Even if the finger is injured, the fingerprint will grow back in the same pattern. For this reason, fingerprints are also called "human ID cards" and are the most special password for each of us.

科学关键词
Science Key Words

指纹： 手指末节内侧表面的皮肤乳突排列而成的花纹结构。

Fingerprint: An impression left by the raised friction ridges of a human finger.

生物识别： 通过计算机与光学、声学、生物传感器等高科技手段的密切结合，利用动物固有的生理特性（如指纹、DNA、虹膜等）和行为特征（如笔迹、声音、步态等）来进行身份鉴定的技术。

Biometric: A technology that uses biological information (such as fingerprint, DNA and iris) and behavioral characteristics (such as handwriting, voice and gait) to identify individuals with the help of computers and high-tech tools such as optics, acoustics and biosensors.

03 蝴蝶的生命周期

Butterfly Life Cycle

你知道吗 Do you know

我们来认识蝴蝶吧！蝴蝶的生命始于卵。蝴蝶通常在树叶上产卵。

经过一段时间，蝴蝶的卵会孵化出幼虫，就是我们通常说的毛毛虫。毛毛虫以树叶为食。

毛毛虫吃啊吃，长得越来越大。当毛毛虫长到足够大时，它们会在自己周围做一个特殊的壳，我们叫它“蛹”。

现在我们知道，蝴蝶的生命周期由 4 个部分组成，即：卵、毛毛虫、蛹 和蝴蝶！

Let's talk about butterflies! Butterflies begin life as an egg.Butterflies lay eggs on leaves.

Baby butterflies are born as caterpillars.Caterpillars eat the leaves.

They eat and eat until they grow much larger.

When caterpillars are big enough, they make a special shell around themselves called a chrysalis.

After many days in the chrysalis, the caterpillar goes through a big change called a metamorphosis.

The caterpillar had changed and comes out of the chrysalis as a butterfly.Then the butterfly will fly off to find food.Finally the butterfly will lay eggs on a leaf to begin the cycle again!

The butterfly life cycle has 4 main parts: egg, caterpillar, chrysalis, and butterfly!

在蛹中度过许多天后，毛毛虫会经历一次巨大的变化，此时毛毛虫从蛹里出来，蜕变为蝴蝶。之后蝴蝶就会飞去寻找食物和伴侣，最终又将卵产在树叶上，开始新一轮的循环！

动手创作吧
Maker Space

我们将制作一个蝴蝶生命周期转盘来展示所学到的知识！
We will make a butterfly life cycle turntable to show what we have learned!

互动小游戏
Interactive Games

其他小朋友说出蝴蝶生命周期的任一阶段或讲述关于蝴蝶生命周期的绘本故事，当你听到蝴蝶生命周期的某个阶段时，请你转动箭头，使箭头指向转盘上对应的阶段。比如，听到蝴蝶，就把箭头指向“蝴蝶”，以此类推。让我们来体验蝴蝶生命周期转盘的乐趣吧！

When the other kids names one of the stages of a butterfly's life cycle or reads a picture book story about it, move the arrow to the matching part. For example, if you hear the word butterfly, move the arrow to the point of "butterfly". Have fun with the butterfly life cycle!

科学小课堂
Science Tips

蝴蝶的翅膀为什么那么绚丽多彩呢？这是因为这些美丽的颜色对蝴蝶来说非常重要哦！有的蝴蝶的颜色可以帮助它们躲藏，让它们的敌人看不见它们；有的蝴蝶的颜色能告诉敌人“我不好吃哦！”；有的蝴蝶的颜色还能帮助它们找到朋友。当阳光照在蝴蝶的翅膀上时，它还会闪闪发光，真是太漂亮了！所以，下次看到蝴蝶时，你就知道它们有多么特别了。

Why do butterfly wings look so colorful? It's because these beautiful colors are very important to them! Some butterflies have colors that help them hide and make them invisible to their enemies, while others warn the enemies, "I'm not tasty." Some butterflies have colors help them find friends. Sometimes when the sunlight shines on the butterfly's wings, they can sparkle! So the next time you see a butterfly, you'll see how special it is.

科学关键词
Science Key Words

生命周期：一个个体从出生到死亡所经历的各个时期。
Life Cycle: The series of changes a person, plant or animal goes through from birth to death.

蛹：完全变态的昆虫由幼虫过渡到成虫的中间阶段的形态。
Chrysalis: A butterfly or moth in the stage between being a larva and an adult.

蜕变：昆虫或两栖类动物幼体在出生或孵化之后的发育过程中发生的一系列内部构造和外部形态的显著变化和急剧改变。
Metamorphosis: A biological process by which an animal physically develops after birth or hatching, involving an obvious and relatively rapid change in the animal's body structure and form.

04 观鸟

Bird Watching

有些鸟有色彩鲜艳的羽毛。有些鸟的羽毛颜色可以帮助它们伪装，隐藏自己。

大多数鸟类能够飞行，但并非所有鸟都具备这种能力。

你知道吗

Do you know

我们周围有各种各样的鸟类。

We see various birds all around us.

Some birds are very large, while others are quite small.

Many birds boast vibrant, colorful feathers.

Some birds use their feather colors for camouflage to blend into their surroundings.

Most birds can fly, but not all have this ability.

Some birds are very big and some are very small.

Do you enjoy bird watching? Scientists who study birds are called ornithologists.

Using binoculars makes bird watching easier, as they magnify your view, allowing you to see further.

有的鸟非常大，有的则很小。

你喜欢观察鸟类吗？研究鸟类的科学家称为鸟类学家。使用双筒望远镜观察鸟类更为方便，它能放大视野，让我们看得更远。

动手创作吧
Maker Space

让我们亲手制作一副双筒望远镜来观察我们周围的鸟类吧！

Let's make a pair of binoculars and watch the birds around us！

互动小游戏
Interactive Games

如果你的朋友和你一起进行了观鸟活动，你们可以在户外宽敞的地方玩“小鸟小鸟飞”的游戏。比如，老师或家长发出口令，“小鸟小鸟飞”，所有小朋友都做飞的动作；“小鸟小鸟游”，所有小朋友都做游的动作，以此类推。口令还可以加上数字，比如“三只小鸟走呀走”，那么小朋友就三人为一组做走的动作，落单的小朋友可以给大家表演个小节目。

If your friends are doing birdwatching with you, you can play "Birdie Birdie Fly" in a large outdoor space. For example, if the teacher or parent says, "Birdie, birdie, fly", all the children will flap their arms like they are flying; if the teacher or parent says, "Birdie, birdie, swim", all the children will move their arms like they are swimming, and so on. It is also possible to add numbers to the command, such as "three birds walk and walk", in which case the children will walk in groups of three.

科学小课堂
Science Tips

鸟为什么能飞呢？这是因为鸟的身体特别适合飞行。首先，鸟的骨头大多是空心的，这样可以减轻它们身体的重量。鸟的胸肌非常发达，这能帮助它们用力地扇动翅膀，给飞行提供充足的动力。鸟的翅膀上覆盖着羽毛，羽毛不仅可以保温，还能让鸟儿身体呈流线型，减少空气阻力。而且，鸟的呼吸系统也很特别，它们的肺和气囊让它们在飞行时呼吸更顺畅。所有这些特点都让鸟成为天空中优雅的飞翔者！

Why can birds fly? This is because birds' bodies are especially suitable for flight. First of all, birds have lighter bodies because the most of their bones are hollow. Birds' allow them to flap their wings with great force and power. The bird's wings are covered in feathers, which not only keep it warm but also give it a streamlined shape and reduce air resistance.

Birds also have a unique respiratory system that enables them to breathe more easily when in flight thanks to their lungs and air sacs. These characteristics enable birds to soar gracefully across the skies!

科学关键词
Science Key Words

伪装：动物通过改变颜色、形状或行为，与周围环境融为一体，以隐藏自己，是一种生存策略。

Camouflage: Animals change their color, shape, or behavior to blend in with their surroundings for protection.

放大：使事物看起来比实际大。

Magnify: The process of making objects appear larger.

鸟类学家：专门研究鸟类形态、分类、习性、和进化等的科学家。

Ornithologist: A scientist who specializes in the study of birds, including their morphology, classification, habits and evolution.

05 植物的部分

Parts of a Plant

植物对维持地球上的生命至关重要。它们不仅是许多动物的食物来源，而且可以通过光合作用释放出我们呼吸所需的氧气。

植物包含树、花和灌木等，一般植物都由以下这几个基本部分组成：

你知道吗

Do you know

今天我们来探索植物的世界。植物有着各种各样的种类、形状和大小，从高大的树到低矮的草，有着丰富的生物多样性。不仅如此，植物的生长环境也非常多样和广泛，有的生长在干燥的土地上，有的则能在水中生长，它们对环境的适应力非常强。

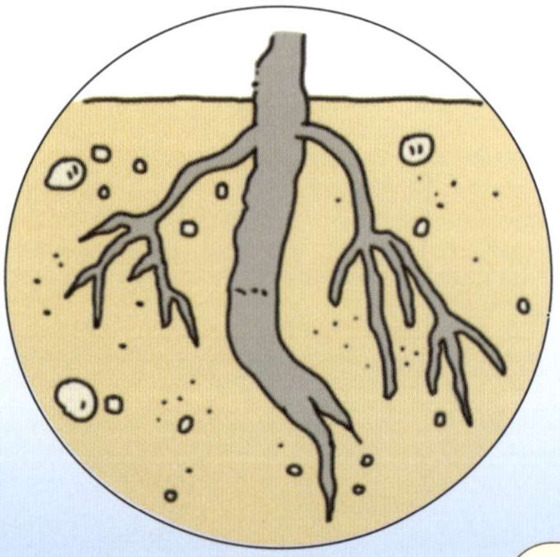

叶子：叶子中的叶绿素能够吸收阳光光能，并通过光合作用将二氧化碳和水转化成葡萄糖和氧气，为植物提供能量。在这个过程中，植物释放出氧气，为地球生态系统贡献了不可或缺的气体。

根：根不仅能吸收土壤中的水分和矿物质，满足植物生长需要，还能稳固植物，防止其因风或水流等外力作用而移位。

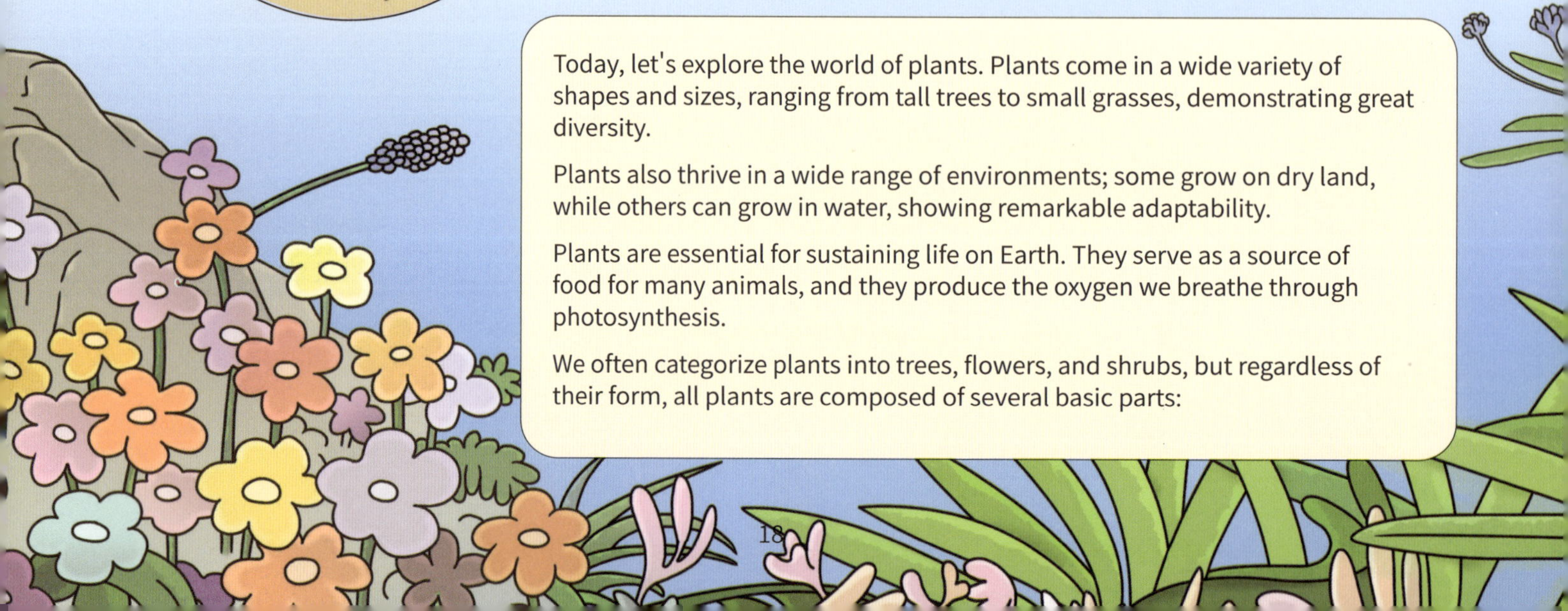

Today, let's explore the world of plants. Plants come in a wide variety of shapes and sizes, ranging from tall trees to small grasses, demonstrating great diversity.

Plants also thrive in a wide range of environments; some grow on dry land, while others can grow in water, showing remarkable adaptability.

Plants are essential for sustaining life on Earth. They serve as a source of food for many animals, and they produce the oxygen we breathe through photosynthesis.

We often categorize plants into trees, flowers, and shrubs, but regardless of their form, all plants are composed of several basic parts:

茎：茎是植物的主要支撑结构，它连接着根部和叶片，支撑着植物向上生长。在树木中，茎就是我们熟知的树干、树枝。

花：花不仅为植物增添美丽，更是繁殖的关键。通过花朵，植物可以结出种子，这些种子随后可以长成新的植物。

Leaves: Chlorophyll in leaves absorb sunlight and convert solar energy into glucose (a kind of suger) and oxygen through photosynthesis, providing energy for the plant. During this process, plants release the important gas, oxygen, into many ecosystems.

Roots: Roots can not only absorb water and minerals from the soil to meet the needs of plant growth, but also stabilize the plant, and prevents displacement caused by external forces such as wind or water flow.

Stem: The stem is the main support of the plant, connecting the roots and leaves, and supporting the plant's upward growth. In trees, the stem develops into what we know as the trunk and the branch.

Flowers: Flowers not only add beauty to the plant, but are also key to reproduction. Through the flowers, plants produce seeds, which can then grow into new plants.

In summary, through the coordinated function of their roots, stems, leaves, and flowers, plants not only beautify our environment but also support and sustain life on Earth. With this knowledge, the next time you are outdoors, you might appreciate the green life around you with more understanding and respect.

总之，植物通过其根、茎、叶和花的协同工作，不仅美化了我们的环境，还维持了地球上的生态系统。了解了这些，下次当你在户外时，会对身边的绿色生命多一份理解和尊重。

动手创作吧

今天，让我们来制作并展示植物主要部分的图片吧！

Today, let's create and display a picutre of the main parts of a plant.

互动小游戏
Interactive Games

其他小朋友说出植物的任何一个部分，请你快速地在你的作品上指出对应的部分。你也可以与其他小朋友交换作品，多次进行互动游戏，进一步熟悉植物的每一个部分。

Other kids name any part of the plant, please quickly point out the corresponding part on your work. You can also exchange works with other children and play interactive games several times to further familiarize yourself with each part of the plant.

科学小课堂
Science Tips

仙人掌为什么没有绿绿的叶子，而是长满了刺？因为仙人掌生活在很少下雨的沙漠里，这里的水非常珍贵。它的叶子变成了刺，这样可以帮助它保存更多的水，不让水分迅速蒸发掉。仙人掌的身体里还能存很多水，就像是它自己的小水壶，让它在干燥的日子里也能开心地生长。这是仙人掌的聪明办法，能帮助它在沙漠里快乐地生活哦！

Why does the cactus not have green leaves, but full of thorns? Because cacti live in deserts where it rarely rains, water is very precious. Its leaves become thorns, which help it to hold more water and prevent it from evaporating quickly. The cactus can also store a lot of water in its body, like its own little kettle, so that it can grow happily on dry days. This is a clever way to help a cactus live happily in the desert.

科学关键词
Science Key Words

氧气： 是人类赖以生存的气体，无色无味。分子式为 O_2。

Oxygen: It is the gas that human beings depend on to survive,colorless and odorless. The molecular formula is O_2.

二氧化碳： 碳或含碳化合物完全燃烧时，或生物呼吸时产生的一种无色气体，是主要的温室气体之一。分子式为 CO_2。

Carbon Dioxide: A colorless gas produced when carbon or carbon-containing compounds are completely burned, or when organisms breathe. It is one of the main greenhouse gases. The molecular formula is CO_2.

光合作用： 绿色植物利用光能将二氧化碳和水同化为有机物（主要是糖类），并释放氧气的过程。

反应式为： $6CO_2+12H_2O \xrightarrow[\text{叶绿体}]{\text{光}} C_6H_{12}O_2+6H_2O+6O_2$

Photosynthesis: Green plants use light energy to assimilate carbon dioxide and water into organic matter (mainly sugars) and release oxygen.

06 彩虹

Rainbow

虹是当光线以一定角度照射到空中的水滴时，光线经过水滴发生折射和反射后，在雨幕和雾幕上形成的彩色圆弧。当我们抬头看天空时，有时会发现红色在外、紫色在内的彩色光带，这就是我们常说的彩虹，彩虹通常出现在雨后。

你知道吗

Do you know

你知道彩虹是怎么形成的吗?

彩虹由七种颜色组成，这些颜色从外圈到内圈依次是:

红色: 如苹果、番茄或者樱桃的颜色。

橙色：如橙子、胡萝卜或者南瓜的颜色。

黄色：如向日葵、小鸡或者香蕉的颜色。

绿色：如草地、树叶或者绿宝石的颜色。

蓝色：如蓝天、蓝鲸的颜色。

这些颜色的记忆方法是：红橙黄绿蓝靛紫。

除了自然形成的彩虹，我们还可以通过三棱镜制造出彩虹效果！棱镜能够模拟光在雨滴中的折射过程，显示出多彩的折射光。

彩虹不仅仅是自然界的奇观，也是光学现象的一个美丽示例。

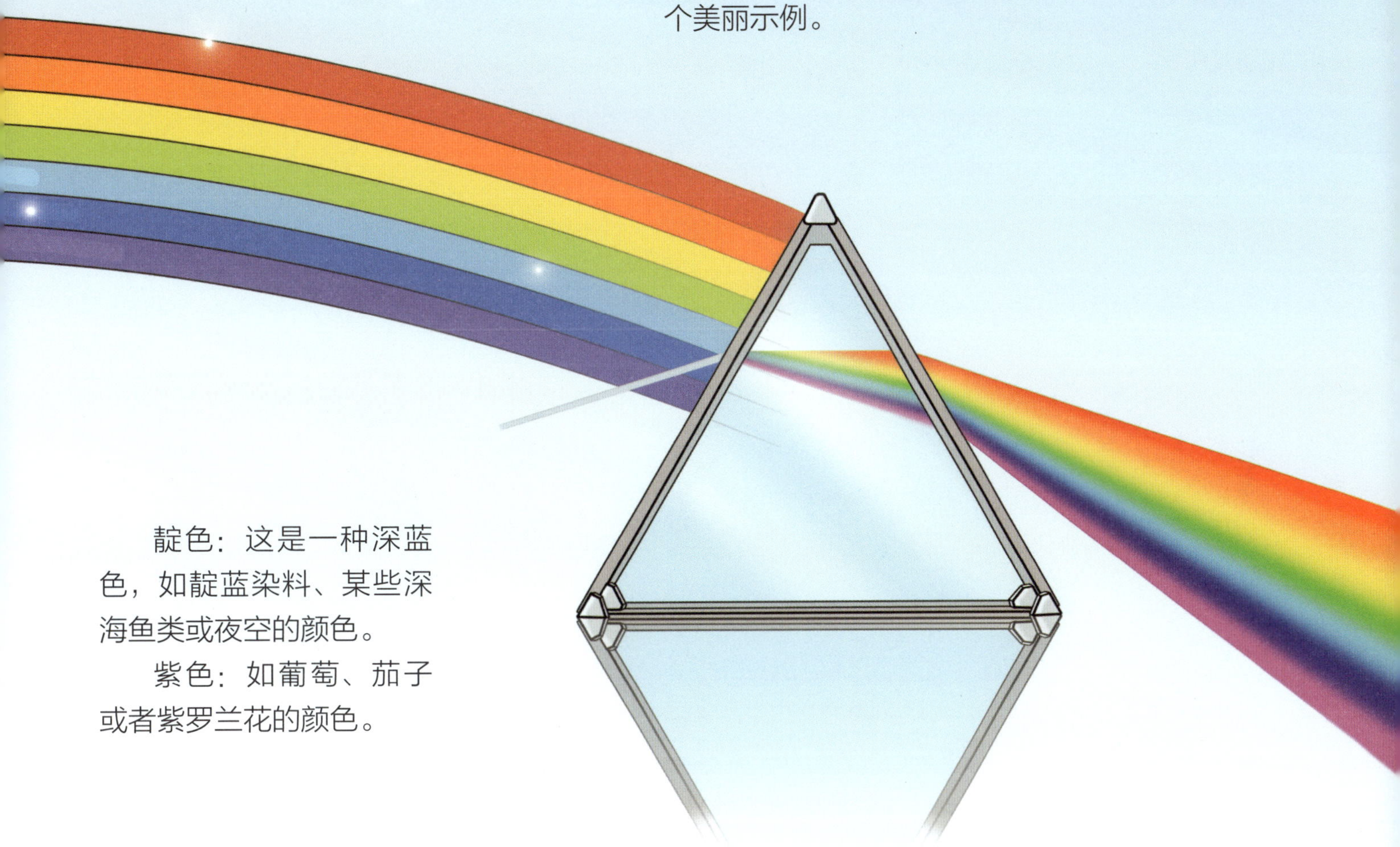

靛色：这是一种深蓝色，如靛蓝染料、某些深海鱼类或夜空的颜色。

紫色：如葡萄、茄子或者紫罗兰花的颜色。

Do you know how rainbows are formed?

When sunlight strikes water droplets in the air, the light is refracted (meaning its direction and speed change due to passing through a different medium) and split into colors, creating the beautiful spectrum of a rainbow. When we look up at the sky, we sometimes find colorful light bands with red outside and violet inside. A rainbow is a colorful arc that appears in the sky, typically seen after rain.

A rainbow consists of seven colors, arranged from the outer to the inner edge as follows:

Red: Like apples, tomatoes, or cherries.

Orange: Like oranges, carrots, or pumpkins.

Yellow: Like sunflowers, chicks, or bananas.

Green: Like grass, leaves, or emeralds.

Blue: Like the blue sky, or blue whales.

Indigo: This is a deep blue color, seen in indigo dye, some deep-sea fish, or the night sky.

Violet: Like grapes, eggplants, or violets.

A mnemonic to remember these colors is Roy G Biv, which represents Red, Orange, Yellow, Green, Blue, Indigo, Violet.

Apart from naturally formed rainbows, we can also create rainbow effects with a prism! A prism can simulate the refraction of light in raindrops, showing the colorful refraction of light.

Rainbows are not only a natural spectacle but also a beautiful example of an optical phenomenon.

动手创作吧 Maker Space

亲手制作属于自己的彩虹吧！

You will make some rainbows!

互动小游戏
Interactive Games

把彩虹的七种颜色，按照从上到下的顺序标注序号，比如红色为 1，橙色为 2，依此类推，紫色是 7。其他小朋友可以任意说出一种颜色或者一个数字，你来回答这种颜色对应的数字或者这个数字对应的颜色。比如，说到“5”的时候，你的答案应该是蓝色；说到“黄色”的时候，你的答案应该是 3。

Label the seven rainbow colors with serial numbers from top to bottom.For example, red is 1, orange is 2, and so on, with violet being 7. Other kids can call out a color or a number, and you must say the matching number or color. For example, when they say 5, your answer should be blue; when they say yellow, your answer should be 3.

科学小课堂
Science Tips

你知道为什么光线照到棱镜能够形成“彩虹”吗？当照到三棱镜上时，光线会分解成许多颜色，分别是红色、橙色、黄色、绿色、蓝色、靛色和紫色，一共七种。这就好像光线穿过了一扇魔法门，变成了一道小小的彩虹。这个过程叫作光的折射。就是这样，棱镜能让我们看到隐藏在光里的所有美丽颜色，就像自然界中的彩虹一样。

Do you know why light passing through a prism creates a rainbow? When light strikes the prism, it divides into seven colors: red, orange, yellow, green, blue, indigo, and violet. It's as if it passes through a magical door and transforms into a tiny rainbow. This is called refraction. Prisms enable us to see all the lovely colors hidden in light, like the rainbow in nature.

科学关键词
Science Key Words

反射： 光波传播到两种介质的分界面时返回到原介质的现象。
Reflection: The return of a light wave from a surface that it strikes into the medium through which it has traveled.

折射： 光波从一种介质传播到另一种介质时，传播方向相对于入射方向发生改变的现象。
Refraction: The bending or turning of a light wave when it passes from one medium to another medium.

三棱镜： 可以把复色光分解成光谱。
Prism: It can decompose polychromatic light into a spectrum.

07 植物的根

Plant Roots

你知道吗
Do you know

在前文中我们提到植物可以利用其根部从土壤中吸取水分和矿物质。那它是如何吸取的呢？

植物的根主要分为直根和须根两类。直根就像一根大吸管，将土壤中的水分和养分吸入植物中。须根由许多较小的根构成，它们像许多小吸管一样从土壤中吸取水分和养分。

根对植物至关重要，因为它们不仅可以吸取水分和养分，还能将植物固定在适当的位置，防止植物倒下或被风吹走。

Previously, we discussed how plants utilize their roots to absorb water and minerals from the soil. So, how does it absorb them?

There are two main types of plant roots: taproots and fibrous roots.

A taproot functions like a large straw, drawing water and nutrients from the soil into the plant.

Fibrous roots consist of many smaller roots, each acting like a small straw to absorb water and nutrients from the soil.

Roots are important for plants not only because they absorb water and nutrients but also because they hold the plant in place, preventing it from falling over or being blown away by the wind.

动手创作吧
Maker Space

我们将探讨植物的根的工作原理，探究直根、须根，或在只有茎的情况下，哪种能更有效地从土壤中吸取水分和养分。

We will look at how roots work and find out if taproots, fibrous roots, or only stems work best for absorbing water and nutrients from the soil.

直根模拟图
Taproot simulation diagram

须直根模拟图
Fibrous root simulation diagram

茎模拟图
Stem simulation diagram

互动小游戏
Interactive Games

植物的根接龙游戏：先尽可能多地了解不同植物的根是直根还是须根，老师或家长指定一种根的种类后，小朋友们可以按顺序接龙回答对应的不同植物，重复者或答不上来者出局，看谁能留到最后。此游戏可重复进行。

Plant roots word chain game: First, learn as much as you can about whether the roots of different plants are taproots or fibrous roots. The teacher or parent says either fibrous root or taproot, and then the children can name a plant that matches. Those who repeat or are unable to answer are out. Let's see who wins at the end. You can play this game over and over.

科学小课堂
Science Tips

你知道哪些植物是直根系，哪些植物是须根系吗？就某一种植物来说，不同植株之间的形态会有一些差异，但它的根系类型是不会改变的，它绝不会由直根系变为须根系，反之亦然。在 20 多万种高等植物中，属于须根系的植物约有 1/4，属于直根系的约占 3/4。

Which plants have fibrous roots and which have taproots? The morphology of different plants varies, but the type of root will remain constant. It will never change from the taproot to the fibrous root, nor from the fibrous root to the taproot. About one-fourth of the more than 200,000 species of advanced plants have fibrous roots, whereas the other three-quarters have taproots.

科学关键词
Science Key Words

营养（植物）： 植物生长发育所需的养分。

Nutrients (Plants): Important substances that help plants grow.

直根： 主根明显发达，垂直向下生长，并发出小侧根的根系。

Taproot: A large,central,and dominant root that grows vertically downward and gives off small lateral roots.

须根： 无明显的主根和侧根区分的根系。大多数单子叶植物的根系为须根系，如小麦、玉米。

Fibrous Root: A root system made up of numerous branching roots of more or less equal length. Most monocotyledonous plants, such as wheat and corn, have fibrous roots.

08 太空宾果游戏

Space Bingo

你知道吗

Do you know

你以前玩过宾果游戏吗？这是一款非常适合与朋友们一起玩的配对游戏。

游戏开始前，指定一位游戏主持人，可以是老师或家长。主持人将念出一组小卡片中不同物品（或数字、字母）的名称。

Have you ever played bingo before? It's a fun matching game that's great for playing with friends.

The teacher or parent should be the game host. The host will call out names of different items from a set of small cards.

Each player will have a large card that features 9 different items. Whenever the host calls out an item that is on your card, cover that item with a token.

If you manage to cover all 9 items on your card, shout "Bingo"! Doing so means you win the game!

Bingo cards are divided into many kinds. Space Bingo are space-themed, with cards featuring comets, Rovers, space stations, rockets, eight planets of the solar system and so on.

每位玩家都会有一张大卡片，卡片上印有 9 种不同的物品。当主持人念出某个物品的名称，而你的卡片上正好印有这一物品时，你就用一个代币覆盖该物品。

当你的卡片上 9 个物品都被覆盖时，大声喊出“宾果”！这样你就赢得了游戏。

宾果游戏卡分为很多种，太空宾果游戏以太空为主题，卡片上有彗星、月球车、空间站、火箭、太阳系八大行星等。

动手创作吧
Maker Space

我们将一起制作一款太空宾果游戏的卡片，并和小伙伴们一起玩！

We're going to make cards and play Space Bingo!

互动小游戏
Interactive Games

除了太空宾果游戏卡，你也可以制作字母宾果游戏卡、数字宾果游戏卡、水果宾果游戏卡、动物宾果游戏卡、植物宾果游戏卡等，让我们一起来享受玩宾果游戏的乐趣吧！

Besides Space Bingo, you could make alphabet, number, fruit, animal, or even plant bingo. Have fun playing bingo!

科学小课堂
Science Tips

你知道宾果游戏的配对其实是基于概率的吗？概率，是用于度量随机事件发生可能性的一个重要数学概念。概率是一个介于 0 到 1 之间的实数，其中 0 表示事件不可能发生，1 表示事件一定会发生，越接近 1，则表示该事件更可能发生；越接近 0，则表示该事件更不可能发生。概率的概念广泛应用于多个领域，包括物理学、统计学和金融学等。在日常生活中，概率也常用于表达某种现象或事件发生或不发生的可能性的大小。

Did you know that the bingo game is based on probability? Probability is an important mathematical term that measures the possibility of a random event occurring. Probability is a real number ranging from 0 to 1, with 0 indicating that the event is unlikely to happen and 1 indicating that the event will happen; the closer it is to 1, the more likely the event is to occur, and the closer it is to 0, the less likely the occurrence. Probability is widely used in a range of fields, including physics, statistics, and finance. In everyday life, probability is frequently used to describe the chance of a phenomenon or event occurring or not occurring.

科学关键词
Science Key Words

彗星： 绕太阳运行的一种质量较小的天体。

Comet: A relatively small celestial body that orbits the sun.

漫游者：用于探索地球以外地方的机器人。

Rover: A robot used to explore places outside of Earth.

望远镜：一种可以让人看到远处事物的工具。

Telescope: A tool that lets you see things that are far away.

09 皮影戏

Shadow Play

你知道吗

Do you know

你看过皮影戏吗？皮影戏在中国有 2000 多年的历史，是中国的优秀传统文化之一。

在皮影戏中，表演者会在幕布后方操控影偶来讲述故事。当灯光从后面照射到幕布上时，影偶会挡住光线，在幕布上形成对应的影子，就像电影放映机那样。

而与电影一样，皮影戏也向我们展示古代和现代的各种故事，例如：讲述英雄的壮举和冒险的故事。

你也可以尝试自己举办皮影戏活动！如果参与人数较多，建议分成每组不超过四人的小组，以确保每个成员都能参与其中。首先，确定你想要讲述的故事。你是想创作一个全新的故事，还是复述一个你已经知道的故事？你选择的故事将决定你需要制作哪些角色、道具或布景。然后，为小组成员分配角色：选择一位负责灯光的放映员，一位负责讲故事或担任旁白的叙述者，其他成员则负责操纵影偶。

Have you ever seen a shadow play?

Shadow play in China has a history of more than 2000 years and is one of the excellent traditional cultures of China.

People move the plays behind a screen to better tell a story.

Light is projected onto the screen, and the plays block the light, creating shadows that mimic the shapes of the plays.

These shadows form images on the screen, similar to how a movie projector creates images on a movie screen.

Like movies, shadow play can share stories from the past and present.

Shadow play can tell tales of great heroes and adventurous stories.

Now, you can try to hold your own shadow play activities too! If there are many participants, it's better to form groups of four or fewer to make sure everyone gets involved.

First, decide on the story you want to tell. Are you going to create a brand-new original story or retell a known story?

The story you choose will determine the characters, props, and scenes you need to create.

Next, assign roles to the group members: Select one person to be the projectionist who controls the light source, another to be the narrator or provide voice-overs, and other members are responsible for manipulating the puppets.

动手创作吧
Maker Space

我们将一起学习如何制作影偶，如何用影偶表演皮影戏，以及如何搭建皮影剧场！

We will learn how to make shadow puppets, how to perform a shadow play, and how to build a shadow play theater!

互动小游戏
Interactive Games

请轮流表演，并在他人演出时做一名合格的观众。

Take turns performing and be a respectful audience when others are performing.

科学小课堂
Science Tips

皮影戏的原理是光的直线传播。具体来说，光源发出的光沿直线传播，在传播过程中被不透明的“皮影”挡住，形成了一片相对较暗的区域，即影子。皮影戏正是利用这一光学原理来完成各种造型和场景的表演。在皮影戏表演中，艺人们使用灯光将角色的剪影投射在屏幕上，从而创造出各种各样的故事和场景。

Shadow play is based on the idea that light travels in a straight line. More specifically, the light from the light source travels in a straight line but is blocked by the opaque "shadow puppet" during the process, leaving a dark area (the shadow). Shadow play uses this lighting technique to create a wide range of roles and settings. In shadow play shows, artists create a lot of stories and settings by projecting silhouettes of characters onto a screen using lighting.

科学关键词
Science Key Words

放映员： 在电影院中操作放映设备，放映影片，并负责设备检查和保养的人员。

Projectionist: A person whose job is to run a movie projector to show films and examine and maintain the equipment.

皮影艺人： 操纵影偶进行表演的人。

Puppeteer: A person who performs with puppets.

布景： 舞台美术的组成部分之一，包括帷幕和投影等。

Scenery: A part of stage art, such as draperies, projection and so on.

道具： 可移动的用于表演的用具。

Prop: A movable object used in a performance.

10 太阳系绳串

Solar System String

你知道吗
Do you know

你以前听说过太阳系吗？你知道这个词是什么意思吗？太阳系是环绕太阳运行的天体构成的集合体及其所占有的空间区域。

在太阳的照射下，地球在不停地自转，所以当地球的一边经历白天时，另一边就是夜晚。

你知道我们的太阳其实是一颗恒星吗？没错，你晚上看到的星星大部分都是恒星，相当于其他太阳系中的太阳。

太阳实际上是一个巨大的燃烧的气体球！科学家估计太阳的表面温度约为5500摄氏度，而它的核心温度则高达 1500 万摄氏度！太阳发出的热量和光线使我们的地球温暖宜居，没有太阳，就没有这个可爱美丽的世界。

我们的太阳系里有多少颗行星呢？答案是八颗行星。

你知道吗？如果一个恒星系中出现多个恒星，就意味着有多个“太阳”。拥有两个“太阳”的多星系统称为双星系统，而拥有三个“太阳”的则称为三星系统。

Have you ever heard of the solar system before? Do you know what that means? The solar system is a group of planets that orbit the Sun ,and the spatial regions they occupy.

Under the Sun's rays, the Earth constantly rotates, making it day on one side and night on the other.

Did you know our Sun is actually a star? That's right, most stars you see at night is a sun in another solar system.

The Sun is essentially a giant ball of burning gas! Scientists estimate that the surface temperature of the Sun is about 5,500 degrees Celsius, while its center can reach temperatures of about 15,000,000 degrees Celsius! The heat and light from the Sun make our planet warm and livable.

How many planets are there in our solar system? There are eight planets.

Did you know that other "solar systems" might have different numbers of "suns"? A "solar system" with two suns is called a binary star system, and one with three suns is called a trinary star system!

动手创作吧
Maker Space

今天我们将用绳子制作一个太阳系模型！

Today we will make a model of our solar system on a string!

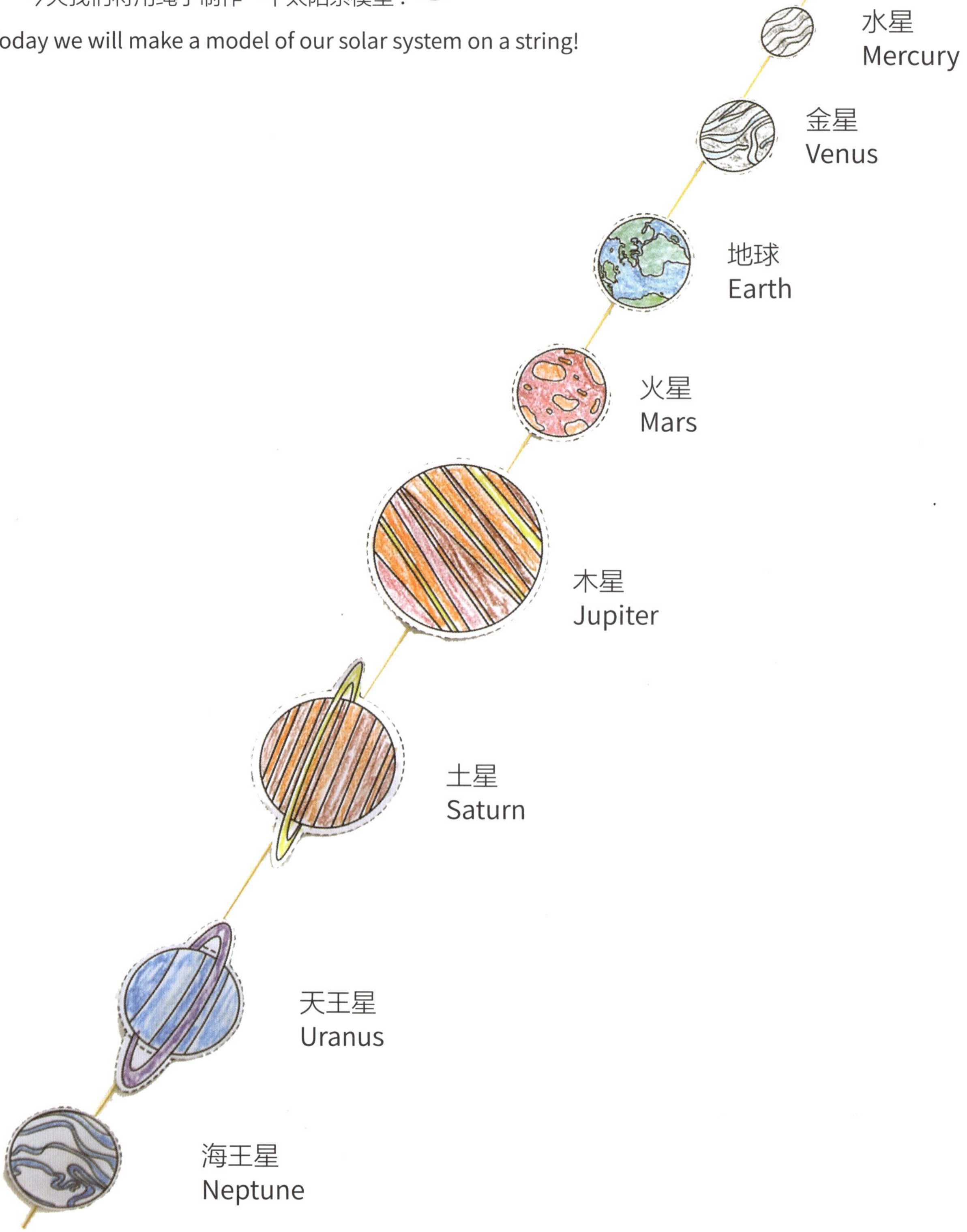

互动小游戏
Interactive Games

让我们按照八大行星到太阳的距离，从近到远地给它们编个号，比如离太阳最近的水星为 1 号，离太阳最远的海王星为 8 号，以此类推。其他小朋友可以说出任一号码或者任一行星名称，你来快速回答对应的行星名称或者号码。比如对方说到“3”，你应该快速回答“地球”；对方说到“土星”，你应该快速回答“6”。这个游戏也可以多人抢答，看谁答得又快又准。

Label the the eight planets with numbers by their distance from the Sun. For example, Mercury is 1, Neptune is 8, and so on. Other kids can call out either number or the name of any planet, and you must say the corresponding number or planet. For example, when they say 3, your answer should be Earth; when they say Saturn, your answer should be 6. This game can also be played by a group to see who can answer quickly and accurately.

科学小课堂
Science Tips

你听说过冥王星吗？以前，人们把它当作我们太阳系的第九颗行星。但是，冥王星真的很小，甚至比月亮还要小一些。2006 年，一群天文学家开了一个会，认定冥王星太小了，不能算作一个真正的行星。所以他们通过投票，把冥王星的等级改成了“矮行星”。这样一来，太阳系就只有八颗行星了。虽然冥王星不再被称为行星，但它仍然是太阳系中一个很有趣的成员哦！

Have you ever heard of Pluto? Pluto was originally called the ninth planet in our solar system!

But Pluto is really small, even a little smaller than the moon. In 2006, a group of astronomers held a meeting and decided that Pluto was too small to count as a real planet. So they voted to change Pluto's status to "dwarf planet". That would leave only eight planets in our solar system.Even though it is no longer considered a planet, Pluto is nevertheless a fascinating part of our solar system!

科学关键词
Science Key Words

太阳系：由太阳和围绕它运动的天体（行星、卫星、小行星、彗星、流星体和行星际介质等）构成的体系及其所占有的空间区域。

Solar System: A system of the Sun and the heavenly bodies orbiting the Sun, including planets, moons, asteroids, comets, meteoroids and interplanetary medium, and the spatial regions they occupy.

轨道：一个物体环绕另一个物体运动的常规路径。

Orbit: A regular path one object takes around another.

旋转：某物绕一点或一轴线作圆周运动。

Rotation: The process of turning around a center or an axis.

11 吸管火箭

Straw Rockets

你知道吗

Do you know

火箭是专为太空旅行设计的交通工具。它们能够搭载宇航员执行太空任务。火箭还用于部署卫星，这些卫星用途广泛，包括电视广播、天气预报、观测地球和全球通信等。此外，火箭还可以把建筑材料和植物、动物等生物运输到太空中。火箭甚至可以到达月球和其他行星。

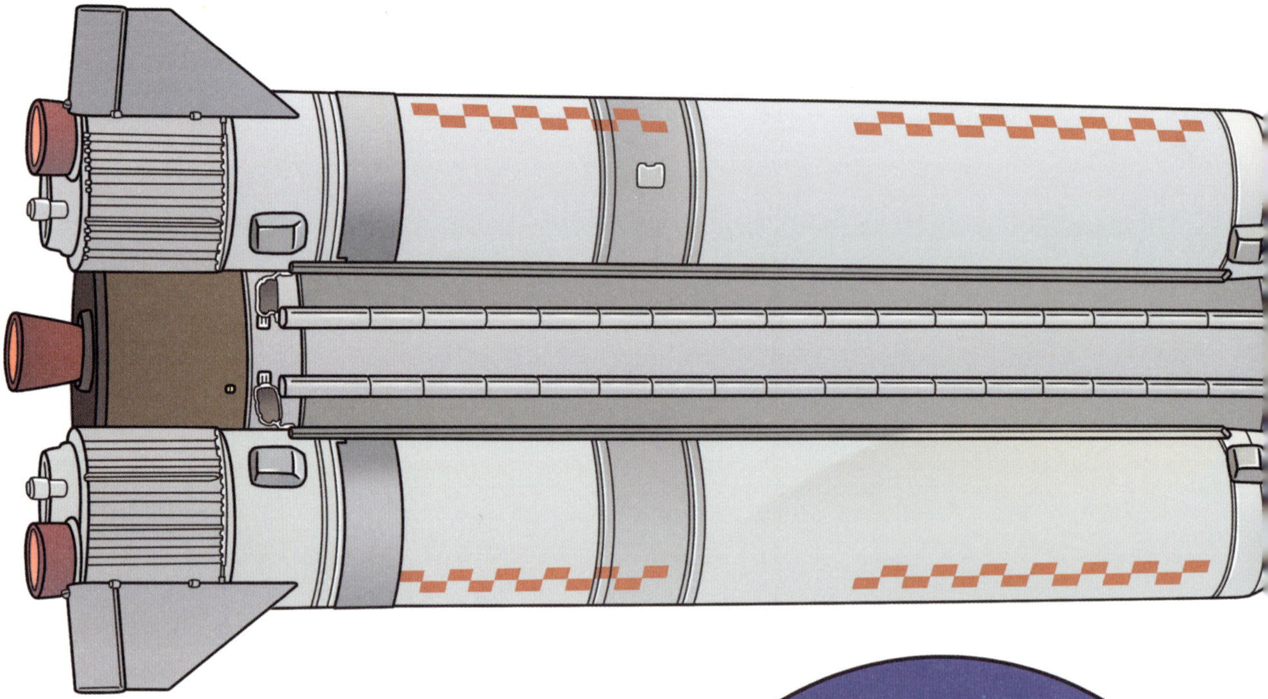

大约 2000 年前，火箭最早在中国被发明出来，最初用于烟花、发射信号、照明等。现代烟花所用的技术仍与这早期设计有不少相似之处。

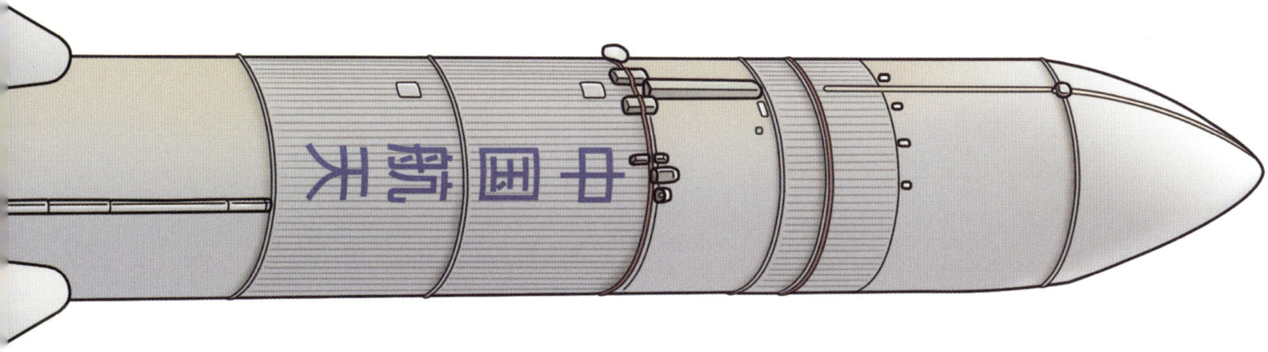

Rockets are vehicles specifically engineered for space travel.

They are able to carry humans, known as astronauts, on space missions.

Rockets also play an important role by delivering satellites into orbit used for TV broadcasting, weather forecasting, earth observation, and global communication.

Rockets have many uses, including the transport of construction materials, and living things such as plants and animals into space.

Rockets can even travel to the moon and other planets.

The earliest rockets, which date back about 2000 years, were developed in China as fireworks. The technology used in today's fireworks still bears a strong resemblance to those early designs.

动手创作吧
Maker Space

我们将一起制作一个吸管火箭并发射它！

We will create a straw rocket and attempt to launch it!

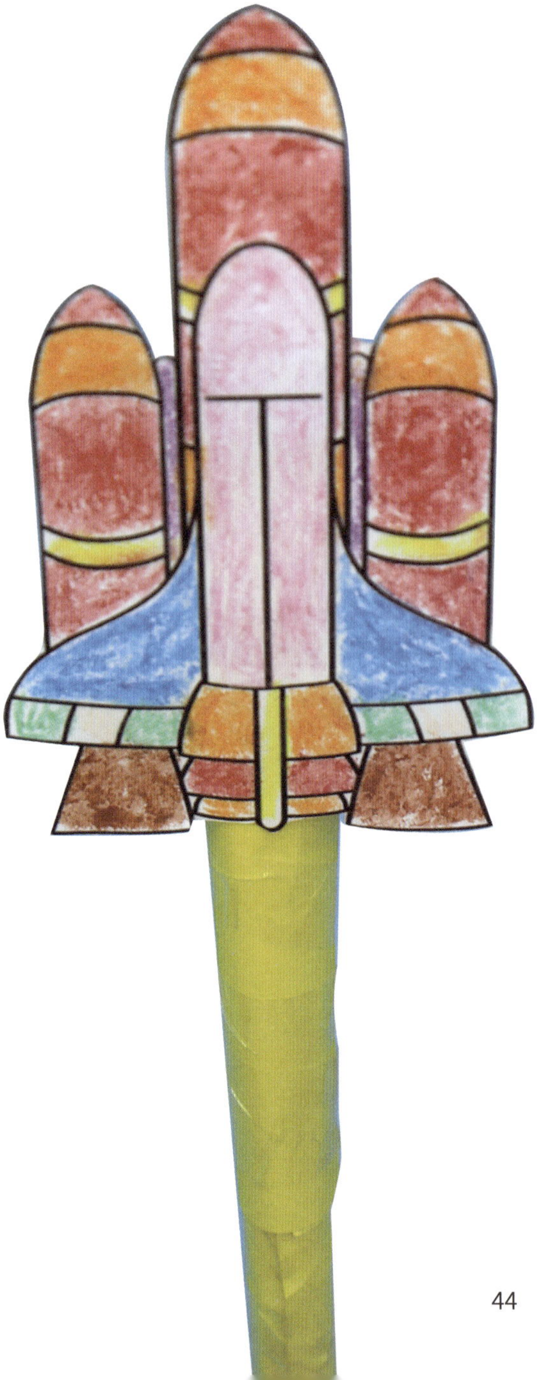

互动小游戏
Interactive Games

你可以和你的朋友们一起玩火箭发射游戏。选定一个火箭发射点，确保每个人在同一个地点发射火箭。一旦每个人都发射了火箭，你就可以拿卷尺测量火箭发射点到火箭着陆地点的距离。如果人数很多，可以测量每枚火箭的射程，或者只测量飞行距离最长的火箭的射程。有时间的话可以多尝试几次！

You can play rocket launch games with your friends. Choose a launch site and make sure everyone launches from the same spot. Once everyone has launched the rocket, you can take a tape measure and measure the distance from the launch site to the landing site of the rocket. If there are a large number of people, the range of each rocket can be measured, or only the range of the rocket that travels the longest distance. If you have time, you can try several times!

科学小课堂
Science Tips

火箭怎么能飞到太空中呢？这都得感谢牛顿发现的两个定律。就像你放开充满气的气球，它会飞走一样，火箭也是这样飞上天的。火箭的燃料燃烧后，气体向下喷出，火箭就往上飞。其原理就是牛顿的第三定律，作用力和反作用力大小相等。火箭要飞出地球，就得有足够的力量克服地球的引力，这需要用到牛顿的万有引力定律。所以，只要火箭推力够大，就能飞到太空中去。

How does a rocket fly into space? It's all thanks to two laws discovered by Isaac Newton. Rockets launch into the sky in the same way that an air balloon takes off when released. When the rocket's fuel burns, the gas ejects, and the rocket goes up. This is based on Newton's third law, which states that the acting force and reacting force are equal. To fly off the Earth, a rocket must have enough force to overcome gravity, which requires the use of Newton's law of gravity. Thus, the rocket can fly into space if it has sufficient force.

科学关键词
Science Key Words

卫星：绕行星运行的单个天体。

Satellite: An object that orbits around a planet in space.

空间站：可供多名宇航员巡防、长期工作和居住的载人航天器。

Space Station: A manned spacecraft served as a base for astronauts to patrol, work and live.

航天器发射：运载火箭运送航天器起飞、加速、进入预定轨道的过程。

Spacecraft Launch: The process by which a rocket sends a spacecraft into the air and the preset orbit with great force.

12 天气转盘

Weather Wheel

你知道吗？

Do you know

天气是一定区域短时间内的大气状态及其变化的总称。研究大气现象的科学家被称为气象学家。

我们会经历许多不同类型的天气。

晴天：太阳高照，天空晴朗。
阴天：天空布满了云，看不见太阳。
雨天：云层厚重，空中的水滴落下来。
雷雨：下雨时会伴随着闪电和雷声。
有风：风力大，树枝会摇晃。
雾：空气中充满了水蒸气，看起来像是白色的烟。
雪：气温很低，天空中飘落下雪花。

The weather is what we call the air or atmosphere around us.

Scientists who study the weather are called meteorologists.

We can experience many different types of weather:

Sunny: The sun shines brightly, and the sky is clear.

Cloudy: The sky is covered with clouds, and the sun is hidden.

Rainy: The clouds are thick, and droplets of water fall from the sky.

Thunderstorms: Sometimes, rain is accompanied by lightning and thunder.

Windy: The wind is strong, and tree branches can shake.

Foggy: The air is filled with water vapor, looking like white smoke.

Snowy: The temperature is low enough, and snowflakes fall from the sky.

Do you know what symbols are used when the weather forecast predicts these kinds of weather?

Which kind of weather do you like the most?

你知道天气预报用什么符号来表示这些天气呢？你最喜欢哪种天气呢？

动手创作吧

我们要一起做一件有趣的事——制作天气转盘！你可以每天转动它来展示出当天的天气。

We are going to do a fun activity — making a weather wheel! You can spin it each day to display the day's weather.

互动小游戏 Interactive Games

拿出你制作的天气转盘，其他小朋友可以说出其中任意一种天气类型，你来移动箭头使其指向这种天气。请给你的同伴尽情展示你知道的所有天气类型吧！你也可以在日历上追踪记录每天的天气情况。月底的时候，数一数这个月有多少晴天、多少雨天等，还可以将统计结果绘制成图表哦。

Take out the weather wheel you've made.Other kids can name any type of weather on the wheel and you spin the arrow to it. Have fun showing your friends all the weather types you know! You can also keep track of the weather each day on a calendar. At the end of the month, count how many sunny days there were, how many rainy days there were, etc. You can also graph the results.

科学小课堂 Science Tips

天气预报是不是每次都很准呢？其实，天气就像是一个非常调皮的小朋友，我们有时候很难猜到它接下来会做什么。因为天气变化涉及很多复杂的东西，就连一点小小的改变都可能让天气发生很大的变化。所以，即使科学家们用了很多高科技设备来预测天气，有时候天气预报还是会有一些不准确的地方。这就是为什么有时候天气预报说有雨，结果却是晴朗无云！

Is the weather forecast always accurate? In fact, the weather is like a very naughty child, and sometimes it is hard to predict what kind of weather it will be next. Because sudden weather changes even minor differences can have significant impact on the weather. This is why weather forecasts are not always correct, even though scientists employ a variety of high-tech equipment to anticipate the weather. That is why sometimes the weather forecast predicts rain but it turns out to be sunny and clear!

科学关键词 Science Key Words

大气层： 泛指地球周围的气体环境。

Atmosphere: The layer of gas or air that surrounds the Earth.

雷暴： 是一种局地性强对流天气。雷暴发生时常伴随有雷击、闪电、强风和暴雨。

Thunderstorm: A storm caused by strong rising air currents and characterized by thunder, lightning, strong wind and heavy rain.